Reading and Writing

Learning Fun Workbook

Published by Highlights Learning • 815 Church Street • Honesdale, Pennsylvania 18431
ISBN: 978-1-68437-924-8
Mfg. 10/2019
Printed in Guangzhou, Guangdong, China
First edition
10 9 8 7 6 5 4 3 2 1

For assistance in the preparation of this book, the editors would like to thank:
Vanessa Maldonado, MSEd; MS Literacy Ed. K–12; Reading/LA Consultant Cert.; K–5 Literacy Instructional Coach
Jump Start Press, Inc.

When They Grow Up

The main idea is what a text is mostly about. Details tell more about the main idea.

Read the text. Answer the questions.

1. What is the main idea?
   - ○ Living things grow up.
   - ○ Living things have different names.
   - ○ Animals and plants are living things.

2. Which is a kind of seed?
   - ○ acorn
   - ○ frog
   - ○ joey

3. How are tadpoles and fawns alike?
   - ○ Both live in water.
   - ○ Both are adult plants.
   - ○ Both are young animals.

4. Draw a line to match each young animal to its parent.

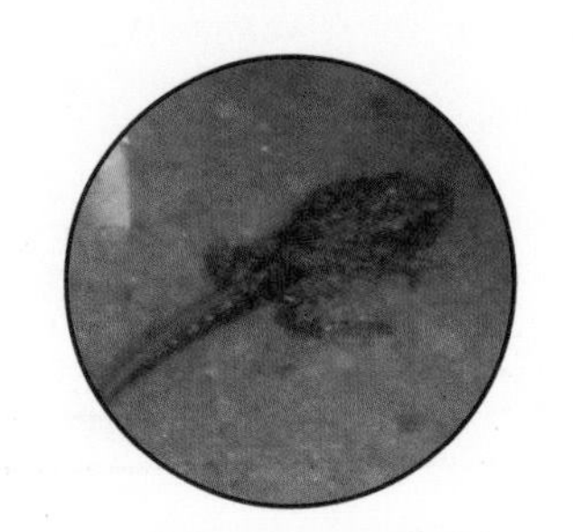

Babies and Parents

Draw pictures that show a young animal and a parent. Below each picture, write to complete the sentence frame.

Title: ______________________________

Written by: ______________________________

A ______________________________

becomes a ______________________________.

A ______________________________

becomes a ______________________________.

Pictures can give extra information.

A ______________________________

becomes a ______________________________.

A ______________________________

becomes a ______________________________.

Can you find 5 differences between these 2 pictures?

Adventures of Spot

"Time to clean up," says Pa.

Spot and Pa work hard.

Pa finds his hammer.

Spot finds his ball.

Time to play!

Characters are people or animals in a story. The setting is where a story takes place.

Read the story. Then answer the questions.

1. Who are the characters?

○ Pa, Ma ○ Pa, Spot ○ Ma, Spot

2. What is the setting?

○ a food store ○ a tool shed ○ a school

3. What happens in the story?

○ Spot and Pa clean up and then play.

○ Spot and Pa make dinner.

○ Spot and Pa build a doghouse.

Write **1**, **2**, and **3** to put the pictures in order.

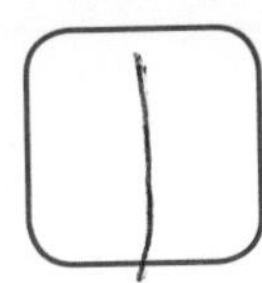

Tell a Pet Tale

Draw pictures that tell a story about a pet. Below each picture, write to tell what happens.

Title: ______________________________

Written by: ______________________________

Pictures can show story characters and events.

Two of these rabbits look exactly alike. Can you find the matching pair?

A Story of Evergreens:

A folktale is a story that has been passed down by storytellers.

Winter was close. It was time for birds to fly away. But one bird hurt his wing. He could not fly. He sat in a maple tree.

"Go away!" said the tree. "It is time for my winter nap."

The oak tree said, "Go away!"

"Hide in my branches," said a pine tree.

"Eat my berries," said a holly tree.

Then Old Frost said, "It is time to start winter."

"I will blow leaves off the trees," said the wind.

"What about the trees that helped the bird?" said Old Frost.

"They have been kind," said the wind. "They may keep their leaves all winter."

A Korean Folktale

Read the folktale. Answer the questions.

1. What do many birds do when winter is close?

fly south.

2. Why didn't the little bird go with the other birds?

he hurt his wing.

3. Why did the wind let the pine and holly trees keep their leaves?

teny were kind.

4. Do you think this is a true story? Why or why not?

no becavse trees dont have faces.

Circle the trees that helped the little bird. Draw a rectangle around the trees that did not help.

MAPLE OAK PINE HOLLY

Word for Word

Shades of meaning tell the difference between words that have almost the same meaning.

Read each underlined word. Write the 2 words from the word box that have almost the same meaning. How are the words different?

branches	broken	glared	hurt	jumped
leaped	looked	small	tiny	twigs

1. One bird had <u>injured</u> his wing.

2. He <u>hopped</u> onto a maple tree.

3. The tree <u>stared</u> at the bird.

4 "Go away, <u>little</u> bird!"

5. "You can snuggle in my low <u>limbs</u>."

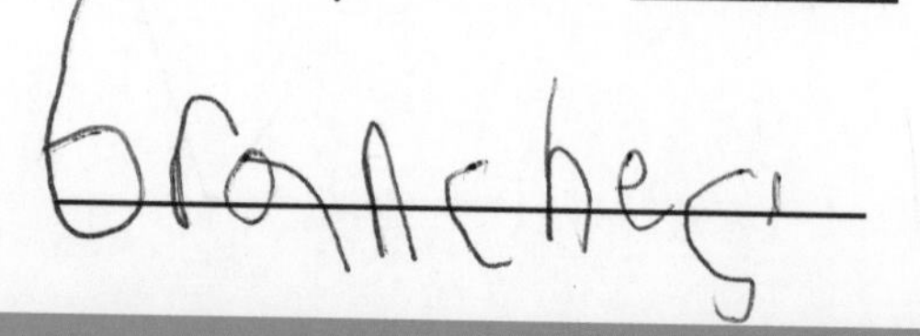

Circle the strongest word in each sentence.

Today is (cold/freezing/cool).

We (slide/skate/glide) on the ice.

She (zooms/rides/moves) down the hill on her sled.

He (flies/soars/lifts) into the air.

That moose is (huge/big/gigantic)!

Our day was (great/amazing/good)!

What silly things do you see?

My Folktale

Think up a folktale of your own. Your story might tell how the giraffe got its long neck. Then complete the story map.

Characters

Setting

Beginning

Middle

End

Write your folktale using the characters and ideas in your story map.

Title: ______________________________

Written by: ___________________________

____

____

____

____

____

____

____

____

____

____

____

____

____

____

L A T E
1 2 3 4

Use the number code above to solve this riddle.
What is a giraffe's favorite type of bedtime story?

Answer: a t a l l t a l e
2 3 2 1 1 3 2 1 4

Meet the Luna Moth

The luna moth is a kind of insect. It has spots on its wings. The spots look like the moon. *Luna* means *moon*. The spots look a bit like eyes, too. The "eyes" scare away animals that try to catch it.

Informational text gives facts that can be proven.

A luna moth grows inside a cocoon. Then it comes out. Its wings are soft and small. They grow wider and harder. The moth can get as big as a man's hand! It is one of the biggest moths.

A luna moth lives up to 10 days. It sips from flowers. But it does not eat. It ate food as a caterpillar. It lives on that food.

Look for luna moths at night. That is when they fly.

Read the informational text. Use the facts from the story to answer the questions.

1. The luna moth is:

○ a reptile ○ an insect ○ a bat

2 *Luna* means:

○ sun ○ one ○ moon

3. The spots on a luna moth's wings can look like:

○ eyes ○ a man's hand ○ a butterfly

4. These wing spots might scare off:

○ a plant ○ an animal ○ a man

5. You might see luna moths:

○ in the morning ○ at lunchtime ○ at night

Draw a line between each insect and its match.

The Life of a Butterfly

Look at each underlined word. Use the context clues—the words and pictures that surround it—to find the meaning.

1. A butterfly **hatches** from a tiny egg.
   - ○ comes out of an egg ○ flies
   - ○ crawls

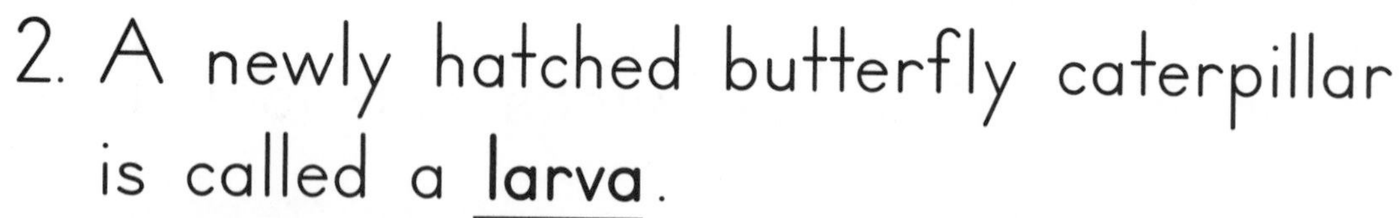

2. A newly hatched butterfly caterpillar is called a **larva**.
   - ○ melted rock ○ young insect ○ moon

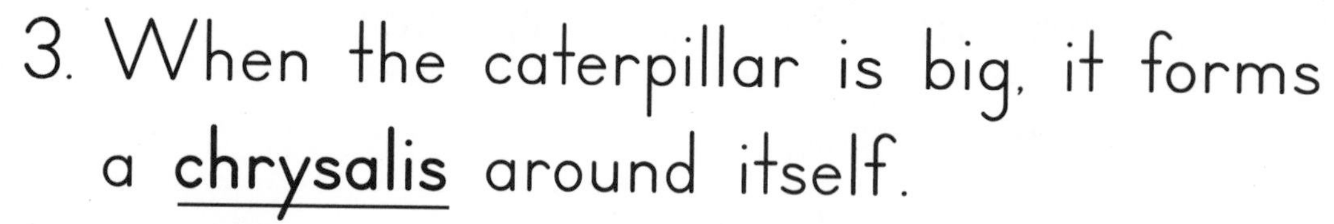

3. When the caterpillar is big, it forms a **chrysalis** around itself.
   - ○ leaf ○ a hard skin ○ wing

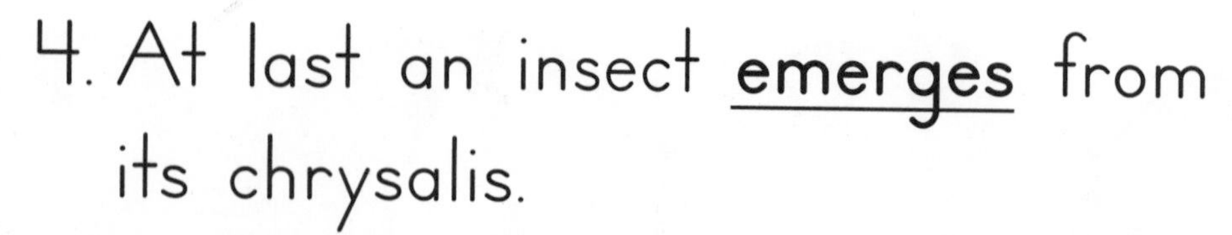

4. At last an insect **emerges** from its chrysalis.
   - ○ sleeps ○ eats ○ comes out into view

5. It has **transformed** from a caterpillar into a butterfly!
   - ○ changed ○ grown ○ fixed

Butterfly House

Use the context clues to fill in each sentence with a word from the word box.

crowded	exclaim	observe	squirms	startled

Our class is visiting an indoor garden. It is ___________ with more than 60 different kinds of butterflies!

Sam is ___________ when one lands on his nose.

I look down and ___________, "One is on my finger!"

Another one ___________ out of its chrysalis.

Ravi uses his magnifying glass to ___________ it.

How many butterflies do you see?

Go Buggy!

An informational paragraph gives facts about a topic.

Get ready to write an informational paragraph about a bug. Complete this text map. Look up facts if you need to.

Topic sentence:

My favorite bug is ______________________.

Detail 1:
What does it look like?

____
____
____
____
____
____
____

Detail 2:
What does it eat?

____
____
____
____
____
____
____

Detail 3:
Where does it live?

____
____
____
____
____
____
____

Closing sentence:

I like this bug because ______________________

____.

Write an informational paragraph. Follow your text map.

Use veggies and cream cheese to make bug-shaped snacks!

Trouble with Tacos

Realistic fiction is a made-up story that could happen in real life.

Ed did not like Taco Tuesdays at school. They always ended with a splat on his shorts or a splurt on the floor.

"Try a soft taco," Max said.

Ed tried one. It was too mushy.

"That taco is too full," Fay said. "Take out the vegetables."

Ed did that. He took one bite. No splat or splurt. But he missed the vegetables.

"Then leave out the meat. Just have the vegetables," Pat said.

Ed tried it. Splurt! He looked at his messy plate. His tummy grumbled. Then he saw the crispy chips.

Yes! Ed knew how to fix his trouble with tacos. He put all the food on top of the chips.

"Yum," Ed said. "Nachos!"

Read the realistic story. Answer the questions.

1. Where does the story take place?

____

2. Why doesn't Ed like Taco Tuesdays?

____

____

3. What did Fay say to try to help?

____

____

4. How did Ed solve his trouble with tacos?

____

____

What differences do you see between these taco trucks?

Pin Down a Problem

Pin up your ideas for a realistic story. Complete this story map.

A good story has a problem and characters who try to solve the problem.

Characters

Setting

Problem: What is wrong?

Solution: How do the characters try to solve the problem?

Write a realistic story. Follow your story map.

Title: ______________________________

Written by: ______________________________

Help Lily solve her problem! Can you find her 12 missing lemons?

Penguin Cup Cozy

A cup cozy keeps drinks hot and protects fingers. Here is how to make one.

A how-to gives step-by-step directions.

You Need

• Scissors • Black sock
• Paper cup • White and orange felt
• Black marker • Glue

1. With an adult's permission, cut off the foot part of a **black sock**. Pull the top part of the sock over a **paper cup**.
2. Cut **white felt** in the shape of a penguin face. Use a **black marker** to draw on eyes.
3. Cut a triangle from **orange felt**. **Glue** the triangle to the face.
4. Glue the face to the sock. Let it dry.

Read the directions and look at the pictures for making a Penguin Cup Cozy. Then write the answers to the questions.

1. What things do you need to make the cup cozy?

2. What do you do with the top of the sock?

3. How do the pictures help you make a shape like a penguin face for Step 2?

4. What is the last step you need to do to finish the cozy?

Step by Step

Write your ideas on how to "build" your favorite craft or your favorite sandwich.

Project

How to ______________________________

You need

____________ ____________ ____________

____________ ____________ ____________

Step 1

____

____

Step 2

____

____

Step 3

____

____

Step 4

____

____

Write your how-to. Follow the ideas you wrote.

Title: ______________________________

Written by: ______________________________

____

____

____

____

____

____

____

____

The Dog and the Bone

A fable is a story that teaches a lesson.

A dog trotted down a path. She had a big bone in her mouth. Then she came to a stream. She looked in the water. There she saw another dog! It had a bigger bone. Yum! That bone looked good.

"Give me that bone!" she growled.

But the other dog did not let go. It held on to its bone.

She opened her mouth to bark. This made her drop her bone. Splash! It fell in the water. It sank out of sight.

The other dog and its bone disappeared, too!

Sadly, the dog trotted home. Now she had no bone at all.

Read the fable. Then answer the questions.

1. How was the dog feeling at the start of the fable?

2. What did the dog see as she crossed the stream?

3. Why did she growl?

4. How did the dog feel at the end of the story?

5. What lesson did you learn from this fable?

These dogs have hidden their bones. How many can you find?

Fable Fun

Think up a fable of your own. Your lesson might be "Slow and steady wins the race" or "Be careful what you wish for." Complete this story map.

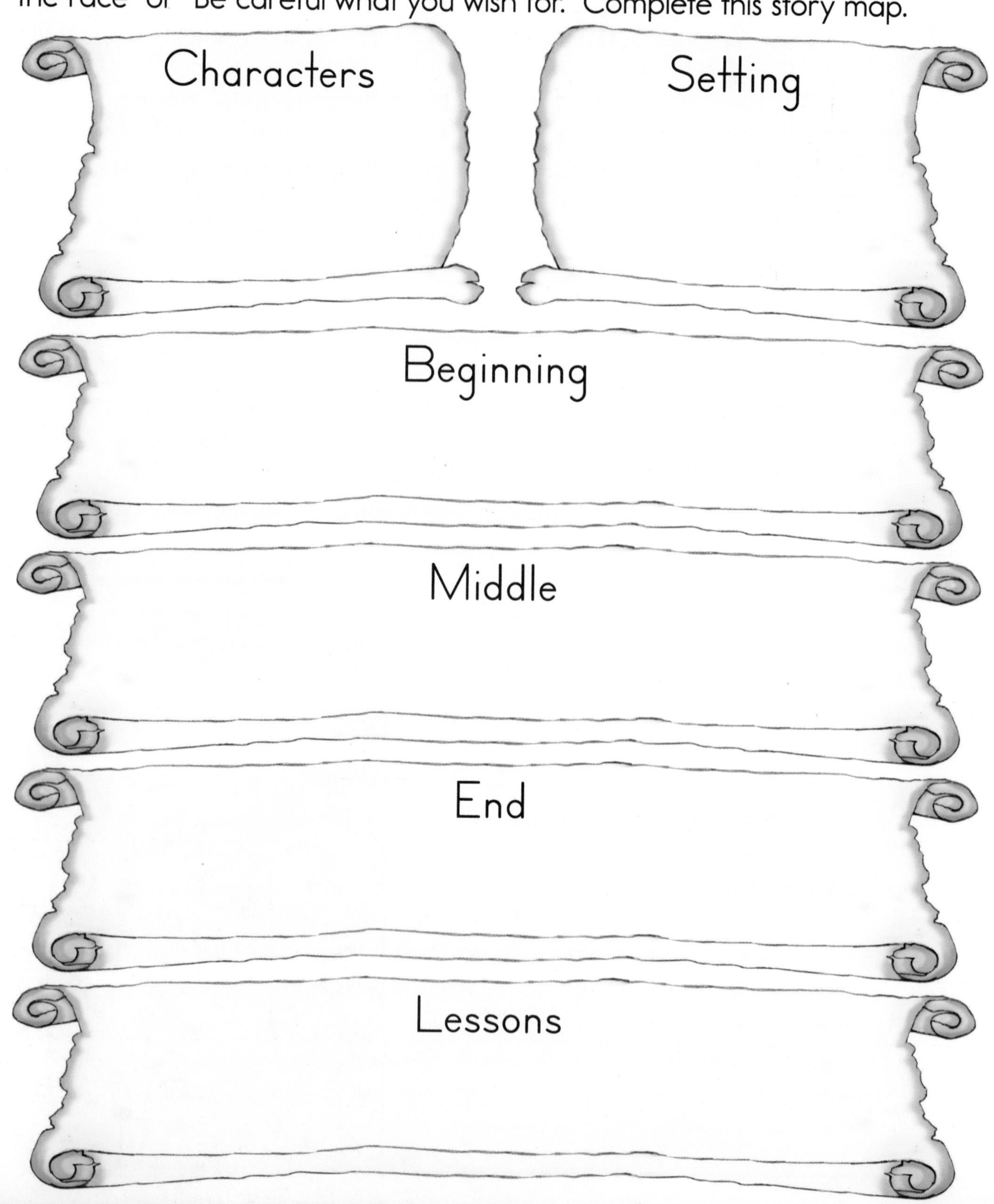

Write your fable from the notes on your story map.

Title: ______________________________

Written by: __________________________

Tortoise or Turtle?

Most tortoises live on dry land. A tortoise has sharp claws. Claws help it dig a hole. It spends most of its time in this hole. That way, it stays out of the hot sun. It comes out to eat plants. It gets water from plants as well as food. A tortoise moves slowly. It hides in its shell if hungry animals come near. Some tortoises live to be more than 100 years old!

Compare to tell how things are alike. **Contrast** to tell how they are different.

Most turtles live near water. A turtle spends most of its time in the water. It has webbed feet to help it swim. Some turtles have flippers. A turtle can hide in its shell. Turtles can live up to 70 years. Turtles eat plants. Turtles also eat meat. They may eat bugs and fish. They may even eat hamburger!

Draw a line from each fact to the correct animal.

Eats plants

Eats meat

Has webbed feet

Lives in dry places

Lives in wet places

Hides in its shell

Can live up to 100 years

Can live up to 70 years

TURTLE

BOTH

TORTOISE

Sort It Out

Sort words by putting them into groups that are alike.

Read the story. Look for words that belong in the same group. Write them in the correct column below.

The boy in the green shirt had a vanilla sundae. The man in the white shorts had mint ice cream in a cone. The clerk made a strawberry shake for a woman wearing a pink hat. Ava dripped chocolate on her new yellow shoes!

Colors	Clothing	Flavors
______	______	______
______	______	______
______	______	______
______	______	______

Find and circle the **5** objects in this Hidden Pictures puzzle.

JO TO S

cane scissors fork envelope flashlight

Write words to describe each animal. Use words from the word bank and other words for color and size.

bird cat flies fur jumps large
legs small spots stripes swims tail

Duck

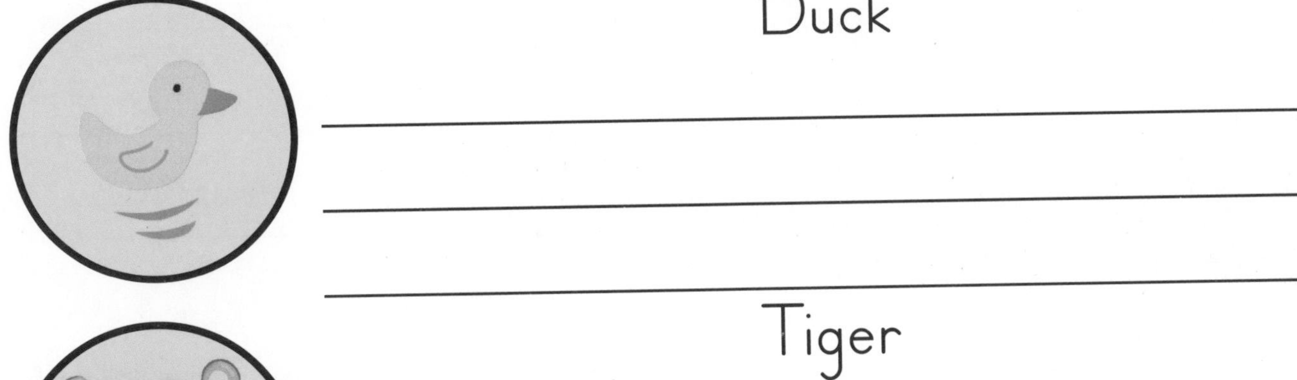

Tiger

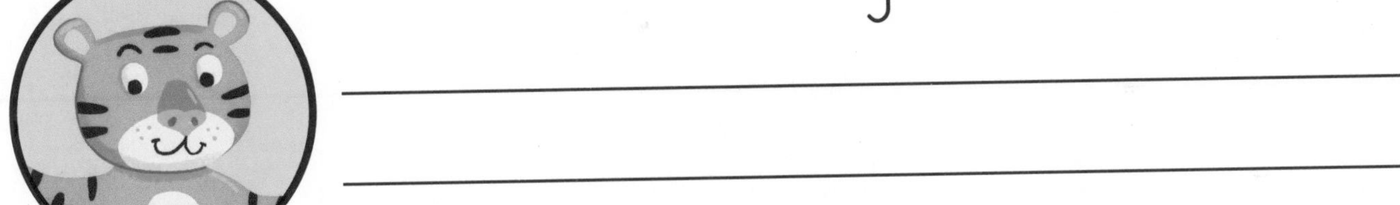

Zebra

Panda

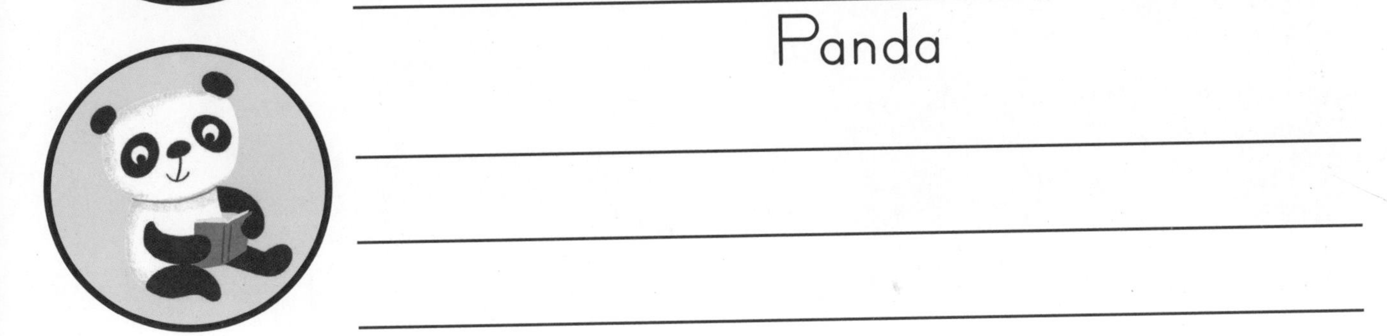

Good Sports

Compare to tell how things are alike. **Contrast** to tell how they are different.

Compare and contrast basketball and tennis. Use the pictures below. Write words in the Venn diagram.

Basketball	Both	Tennis
____________	____________	____________
____________	____________	____________
____________	____________	____________
____________	____________	____________
____________	____________	____________
____________	____________	____________
____________	____________	____________
____________	____________	____________

Basketball

Tennis

Write a paragraph that compares and contrasts basketball and tennis. Use ideas from your Venn diagram.

A City Rap

A poem uses words to make a reader feel a certain way or to paint pictures in a reader's mind.

As I'm walking down the street,
I click my fingers to the beat.
Car horns beep and tires skid;
I hit the top of a metal lid.
Babies cry, a cell phone rings;
I tap my feet to the sound of things.
Children shout in a noisy crowd;
I hum the rhythm and laugh out loud.
Litter crinkles, puddles plop;
I knock the wall—I cannot stop.
As I am walking down the street,
I click my fingers to the beat.

Read the poem. Then answer the questions.

1. How does the boy feel as he is walking?

○ sad ○ happy ○ angry

2. Write a word from the poem that rhymes with *crowd*.

____

3. What sounds does the boy hear?

____

____

4. What things does the poem help you see?

____

____

5. How does this poem make you feel? Which words in the poem make you feel that way?

____

____

____

Spelling Feelings

Read the story below. Circle each word that describes a feeling.

Some feelings are happy, sad, silly, or angry.

Tom was tired. It was the day of the spelling bee. He had worked hard to get ready. His friend Pam said she felt happy. But Tom was worried. What if he made a big mistake? He was also a bit sad. His grandma lived too far away to come. He wished she could be there.

Then his name was called. Tom felt shaky when he got his first word to spell. But soon he was happy. He was able to spell "shaky"!

Later, Tom missed a word. He did not win the bee. He felt sad. But his parents were still proud of him. Even better, he saw Grandma! She had made it to the bee!

This Makes Sense!

Use your five senses! Write the words from the word box that best fit each sense column. Some words might fit more than one sense. But write each word only once.

Some words tell how things look, smell, sound, feel, or taste.

bright	creaky	crunchy				
dark	fluffy	fresh	heavy	juicy	quiet	
rotten	scary	sharp	sour	squeaky	stinky	

It looks

____________ ____________ ____________

It smells

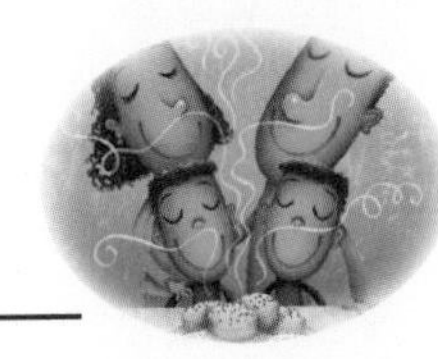

____________ ____________ ____________

It sounds

____________ ____________ ____________

It feels

____________ ____________ ____________

It tastes

____________ ____________ ____________

Now read the poem on page 40 again. Circle the words that describe sounds.

Read All About It

A book report gives the book's title, author, characters, and the main idea of the story. It gives an opinion by the reader and reasons for that opinion.

Read this book report. Underline the title, then circle the author's name. Underline the reader's opinion, then circle the reasons for that opinion.

An opinion is what a person thinks about something. A reason tells why the person thinks a certain way.

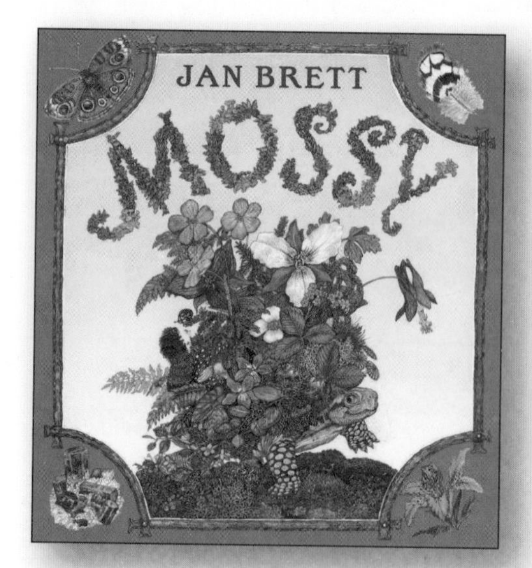

My favorite book is *Mossy* by Jan Brett. It is about a turtle who grows plants on her shell. My favorite part is when she starts to grow a garden on her shell. I love this book because I love turtles and plants.

Can you say this tongue twister five times fast?

BENNY BETTA BUYS A BOOK.

My Favorite Book

Write a book report about your favorite book.

Highlights

FIRST GRADE 1

Congratulations!

____

(your name)

worked hard
and finished the

Reading and Writing

Learning Fun Workbook

Answers

Inside Front Cover

Page 3
When They Grow Up

Which is a kind of seed?
acorn

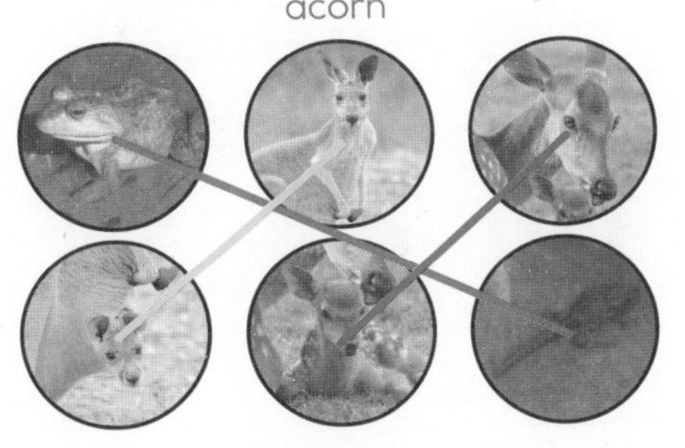

Page 5
Babies and Parents

Page 7
Adventures of Spot

1. Who are the characters? Pa, Spot
2. What is the setting? a tool shed
3. What happens in the story?
   Spot and Pa clean up and then play.

3 1 2

Page 9
Tell a Pet Tale

Page 11
A Korean Folktale

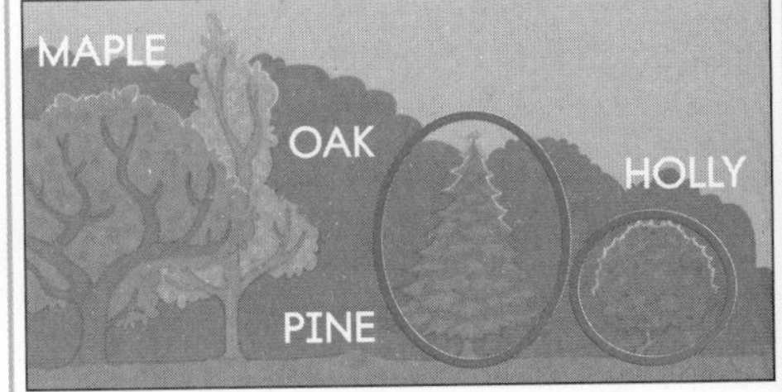

Page 12
Word for Word

One bird had injured his wing.
broken hurt

He hopped onto a maple tree.
jumped leaped

The tree stared at the bird.
looked glared

"Go away, little bird!"
small tiny

"You can snuggle in my low limbs."
twigs branches

Page 13
Word for Word

Today is (cold/freezing/cool).

We (slide/skate/glide) on the ice.

She (zooms/rides/moves) down the hill on her sled.

He (flies/soars/lifts) into the air.

That moose is (huge/big/gigantic)!

Our day was (great/amazing/good)!

Page 15
My Folktale

What is a giraffe's favorite type of bedtime story?

A TALL TALE

Page 17
Meet the Luna Moth

Page 17
Meet the Luna Moth

1. The luna moth is: an insect
2 Luna means: moon
3. The spots on a luna moth's wings can look like: eyes
4. These wing spots might scare off: an animal
5. You might see luna moths: at night

Page 18
The Life of a Butterfly

1. A butterfly **hatches** from a tiny egg. comes out of an egg
2. A newly hatched butterfly caterpillar is called a **larva**. young insect
3. When the caterpillar is big, it forms a **chrysalis** around itself. a hard skin
4. At last an insect **emerges** from its chrysalis. comes out into view
5. It has **transformed** from a caterpillar into a butterfly! changed

Page 19
Butterfly House

Our class is visiting an indoor garden. It is crowded with more than 60 different kinds of butterflies!

Sam is startled when one lands on his nose.

I look down and exclaim, "One is on my finger!"

Another one squirms out of its chrysalis.

Ravi uses his magnifying glass to observe it.

Answers

Page 19
Butterfly House

8 BUTTERFLIES

Page 23
Trouble with Tacos

Page 25
Pin Down a Problem

Page 27
Penguin Cup Cozy

1. You need scissors, a black sock, a paper cup, white and orange felt, a black marker, glue.
2. Pull the top part of the sock over a paper cup.
3. You can use the picture at the bottom to see how face is shaped.
4. Glue the face to the sock. Let it dry.

Page 29
Step by Step

Page 31
The Dog and the Bone

Page 31
The Dog and the Bone

1. How was the dog feeling at the start of the fable? Happy he had a bone.
2. What did the dog see as she crossed the stream? Another dog.
3. Why did she growl? The dog had a bigger bone.
4. How did the dog feel at the end of the story? Sad he had no bone.
5. What lesson did you learn from this fable? Jealousy dosen't pay.

Page 35
Tortoise or Turtle?

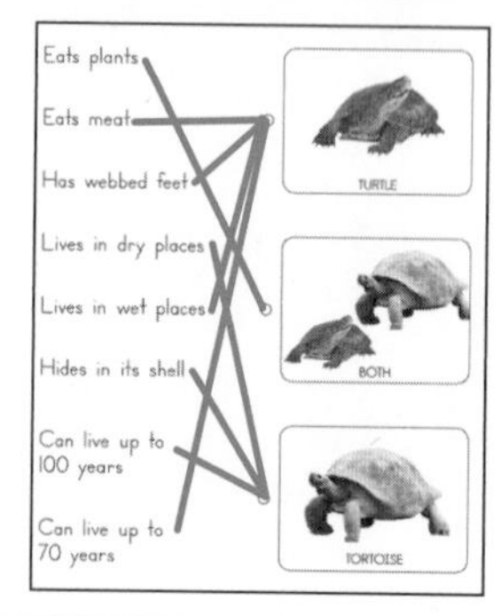

Page 36
Sort It Out

Colors	Clothing	Flavors
GREEN	SHIRT	VANILLA
WHITE	SHORTS	MINT
PINK	HAT	STRAWBERRY
YELLOW	SHOES	CHOCOLATE

Page 41
A City Rap

1. How does the boy feel as he is walking? happy
2. Write a word from the poem that rhymes with crowd. loud
3. What sounds does the boy hear? car horns beep, tires skid, babies cry, cell phone rings, children shout, litter crinkles, puddles plop
4. What things does the poem help you see? the city neighborhood

Page 42
Spelling Feelings

Tom was tired. It was the day of the spelling bee. He had worked hard to get ready. His friend Pam said she felt happy. But Tom was worried. What if he made a big mistake? He was also a bit sad. His grandma lived too far to come. He wished she could be there.

Then his name was called. Tom felt shaky when he got his first word to spell. But soon he was happy. He was able to spell "shaky"!

Later, Tom missed a word. He did not win the bee. He felt sad. But his parents were still proud of him. Even better, he saw Grandma! She had made it to the bee!